W9-AAX-457

Teacher

Published in the United States by
QEB Publishing, Inc.
3 Wrigley, Suite A
Irvine, CA 92618

www.qeb-publishing.com

Library of Congress Cataloging-in-Publication Data

Askew, Amanda.
   Teacher / by Amanda Askew ; illustrated by
Andrew Crowson.
         p. cm. -- (QEB people who help us)
   ISBN 978-1-59566-991-9 (hardcover)
  1. Teachers--Juvenile literature. I. Crowson,
Andrew, ill. II. Title.
   LB1775.A73 2010
   371.1--dc22

2009001991

Printed and bound in China

Words in bold are explained in the glossary on page 24.

Author Amanda Askew
Designer and Illustrator Andrew Crowson
Consultants Shirley Bickler and Tracey Dils

Publisher Steve Evans
Creative Director Zeta Davies
Managing Editor Amanda Askew

Teacher

Amanda Askew
Andrew Crowson

QEB

QEB Publishing

Meet Kimi. She's a teacher at Nuttfield School. She teaches five and six year olds.

When Kimi arrives at the school, Bob the **janitor** is sweeping the **playground**.

Carol the school **secretary** is getting the **attendances** ready for the day.

Peter the **principal** is chatting to another teacher.

At 9 o'clock, the pupils arrive and they're noisy!

"Quiet! It's time for attendance. Good morning."

"Good morning, Miss Nakata."

Kimi uses a check for children who are here and an 'A' for **absent** when children are ill.

Monday February 23rd

Morning · Math
Science

Afternoon · Literacy

"I've written today's **timetable** on the **whiteboard**. This morning, we're going to add money."

"On the table, there are pennies, nickels, and dimes. How many different ways can you add them together to make 20 cents?"

Kimi and Miss Jennings, Kimi's assistant, walk around the room and help the children.

"Miss Nakata, I've finished."
"How many different ways do you have, Robert?"
"I've found eight ways."
"Well done!"

RING! RING! Playtime!

It's raining outside, so Kimi tells the children to play quietly inside. Jane and Lisa play with their teddies.

Jonathan and Joe build towers with play-bricks.

Claire, Alice, and May look at a book about scary animals.

After playtime,
Kimi and the
children plant
beans. They fill
a small pot with
soil. Then they
plant a bean
and add water.

"Put some pots next to the window and some in the cupboard. Then we can see which grows best."

RING! RING! Lunchtime!

Kimi eats her lunch with the children. Some children bring lunch from home. Jack has a cheese sandwich, a yogurt, and a banana.

Some children have
school lunches.

May has pasta
with mushrooms,
sweetcorn, ham,
and broccoli.

In the
afternoon,
Kimi reads
the children
a story.

The story is about a mouse that lives in a lighthouse.

"I need to help my friend," Kimi squeaks in her best mouse voice. All the children laugh!

"What do you know about mice?"

"They are very small."
"They have whiskers and a long tail."
"My pet mouse is called Ralph."

"Excellent. Now, draw a mouse on your piece of paper and write a story about your mouse's adventures!"

"Well done! You've worked very hard today."

"Miss Jennings will put your pictures on the wall and we can sing a song before the bell rings."

"Hickory dickory dock,
the mouse ran up the clock.
The clock struck one,
the mouse ran down,
hickory dickory dock!"

Glossary

Absent Not at school.

Attendance A list of names, so the teacher can check who is at school and who is absent.

Janitor The person who looks after the school building and makes sure it is clean and tidy.

Playground An area outside where children play.

Principal The teacher who is in charge of the school.

Secretary The person who looks after all the school files and attendance.

Timetable A list of what happens each day in a class.

Whiteboard A board on the wall that teachers write on using a special pen.